September 2018

Sunday	Monday	Tuesday	Wednesday	Thursday	Friday	Saturday
						1
2	3 Labor Day	4	5	6	7	8
9 Rosh Hashanah begins at sundown Grandparents Day	10 Islamic New Year begins at sundown	11	12	13	14	15
16	17	18 Yom Kippur begins at sundown	19	20	21 International Day of Peace	22
23 / 30	24 Queen's Birthday (WA Australia)	25	26	27	28	29

October 2018

Sunday	Monday	Tuesday	Wednesday	Thursday	Friday	Saturday
	1 Labour Day (ACT, NSW & SA Australia) Queen's Birthday (QLD Australia)	2	3	4	5	6
7	8 Columbus Day Observed Thanksgiving (Canada)	9	10	11	12 Traditional Columbus Day	13
14	15	16	17	18	19	20
21	22 Labour Day (New Zealand)	23	24	25	26	27
28	29	30	31 Halloween			

W0259627

November 2018

Sunday	Monday	Tuesday	Wednesday	Thursday	Friday	Saturday
				1	2	3
4 U.S. Daylight Saving Time ends at 2:00 a.m.	5	6 Election Day	7	8	9	10
11 Veterans Day Remembrance Day (Canada)	12	13	14	15	16	17
18	19 Mawlid an-Nabi begins at sundown	20	21	22 Thanksgiving	23	24
25	26	27	28	29	30	

December 2018

Sunday	Monday	Tuesday	Wednesday	Thursday	Friday	Saturday
						1
2 Hanukkah begins at sundown	3	4	5	6	7	8
9	10	11	12	13	14	15
16	17	18	19	20	21	22
23 / 30	24 / 31	25 Christmas	26 Kwanzaa Boxing Day	27	28	29

The world
is its own magic.
—Shunryu Suzuki

January

2019

Sunday	Monday	Tuesday	Wednesday	Thursday	Friday	Saturday
		1 New Year's Day	2 Bank Holiday (Scotland & New Zealand)	3	4	5
6	7	8	9	10	11	12
13	14	15 Martin Luther King Jr.'s Birthday	16	17	18	19
20	21 Martin Luther King Day	22	23	24	25	26 Australia Day (Australia)
27	28	29	30	31		

DECEMBER 2018

S	M	T	W	Th	F	S
						1
2	3	4	5	6	7	8
9	10	11	12	13	14	15
16	17	18	19	20	21	22
23/30	24/31	25	26	27	28	29

FEBRUARY 2019

S	M	T	W	Th	F	S
					1	2
3	4	5	6	7	8	9
10	11	12	13	14	15	16
17	18	19	20	21	22	23
24	25	26	27	28		

February 2019

Sunday	Monday	Tuesday	Wednesday	Thursday	Friday	Saturday
					1	2
3	4	5 Lunar New Year	6 Waitangi Day (New Zealand)	7	8	9
10	11	12 Lincoln's Birthday	13	14 Valentine's Day	15	16
17	18 Presidents Day	19	20	21	22 Washington's Birthday	23
24	25	26	27	28		

JANUARY 2019

S	M	T	W	TH	F	S
		1	2	3	4	5
6	7	8	9	10	11	12
13	14	15	16	17	18	19
20	21	22	23	24	25	26
27	28	29	30	31		

MARCH 2019

S	M	T	W	TH	F	S
					1	2
3	4	5	6	7	8	9
10	11	12	13	14	15	16
17	18	19	20	21	22	23
24/31	25	26	27	28	29	30

The only Zen
you can find
on the tops
of mountains
is the Zen you
bring up there.
–Robert Pirsig

The meaning of life is to see. —Huineng

FEBRUARY 2019

S	M	T	W	TH	F	S
					1	2
3	4	5	6	7	8	9
10	11	12	13	14	15	16
17	18	19	20	21	22	23
24	25	26	27	28		

APRIL 2019

S	M	T	W	TH	F	S
	1	2	3	4	5	6
7	8	9	10	11	12	13
14	15	16	17	18	19	20
21	22	23	24	25	26	27
28	29	30				

Sunday	Monday	Tuesday	Wednesday	Thursday	Friday	Saturday
					1	2
3	4 Labour Day (WA Australia)	5	6 Ash Wednesday	7	8	9
10 U.S. Daylight Saving Time begins at 2:00 a.m.	11 Labour Day (VIC Australia)	12	13	14	15	16
17 St. Patrick's Day	18	19	20	21	22	23
24	25	26	27	28	29	30
31						

March

2019

Zen is your everyday thought. —Chao-chou

April

2019

Sunday	Monday	Tuesday	Wednesday	Thursday	Friday	Saturday
	1	2 Lailat al Miraj begins at sundown	3	4	5	6
7	8	9	10	11	12	13
14 Palm Sunday	15	16	17	18	19 Good Friday Passover begins at sundown	20
21 Easter	22 Earth Day Easter Monday Bank Holiday (Eng., Wales, N. Ire., Austral., N.Z.)	23	24	25 Anzac Day (Australia & New Zealand)	26	27
28	29	30				

MARCH 2019

S	M	T	W	Th	F	S
					1	2
3	4	5	6	7	8	9
10	11	12	13	14	15	16
17	18	19	20	21	22	23
24/31	25	26	27	28	29	30

MAY 2019

S	M	T	W	Th	F	S
			1	2	3	4
5	6	7	8	9	10	11
12	13	14	15	16	17	18
19	20	21	22	23	24	25
26	27	28	29	30	31	

May 2019

Sunday	Monday	Tuesday	Wednesday	Thursday	Friday	Saturday
APRIL 2019	JUNE 2019		1	2	3	4
5 Ramadan begins at sundown	6 Bank Holiday (United Kingdom) Labour Day (QLD Australia)	7	8	9	10	11
12 Mother's Day	13	14	15	16	17	18
19	20 Victoria Day (Canada)	21	22	23	24	25
26	27 Memorial Day Observed Spring Bank Holiday (United Kingdom)	28	29	30 Traditional Memorial Day	31	

APRIL 2019

S	M	T	W	Th	F	S
	1	2	3	4	5	6
7	8	9	10	11	12	13
14	15	16	17	18	19	20
21	22	23	24	25	26	27
28	29	30				

JUNE 2019

S	M	T	W	Th	F	S
						1
2	3	4	5	6	7	8
9	10	11	12	13	14	15
16	17	18	19	20	21	22
23/30	24	25	26	27	28	29

For everything that lives is
holy, life delights in life.
—William Blake

You are the sky. Everything
else—it's just the weather.
—Pema Chödrön

Sunday	Monday	Tuesday	Wednesday	Thursday	Friday	Saturday
						1
2	3 Queen's Birthday (New Zealand)	4 Eid al-Fitr begins at sundown	5	6	7	8
9	10 Queen's Birthday (Australia exc. QLD & WA)	11	12	13	14 Flag Day	15
16 Father's Day	17	18	19	20	21	22
23 / 30	24 St. Jean Baptiste Day (Canada)	25	26	27	28	29

MAY 2019

S	M	T	W	TH	F	S
			1	2	3	4
5	6	7	8	9	10	11
12	13	14	15	16	17	18
19	20	21	22	23	24	25
26	27	28	29	30	31	

JULY 2019

S	M	T	W	TH	F	S
	1	2	3	4	5	6
7	8	9	10	11	12	13
14	15	16	17	18	19	20
21	22	23	24	25	26	27
28	29	30	31			

June 2019

July 2019

Sunday	Monday	Tuesday	Wednesday	Thursday	Friday	Saturday
	1 Canada Day (Canada)	2	3	4 Independence Day	5	6
7	8	9	10	11	12	13
14	15	16	17	18	19	20
21	22	23	24	25	26	27
28	29	30	31			

JUNE 2019

S	M	T	W	Th	F	S
						1
2	3	4	5	6	7	8
9	10	11	12	13	14	15
16	17	18	19	20	21	22
23/30	24	25	26	27	28	29

AUGUST 2019

S	M	T	W	Th	F	S
				1	2	3
4	5	6	7	8	9	10
11	12	13	14	15	16	17
18	19	20	21	22	23	24
25	26	27	28	29	30	31

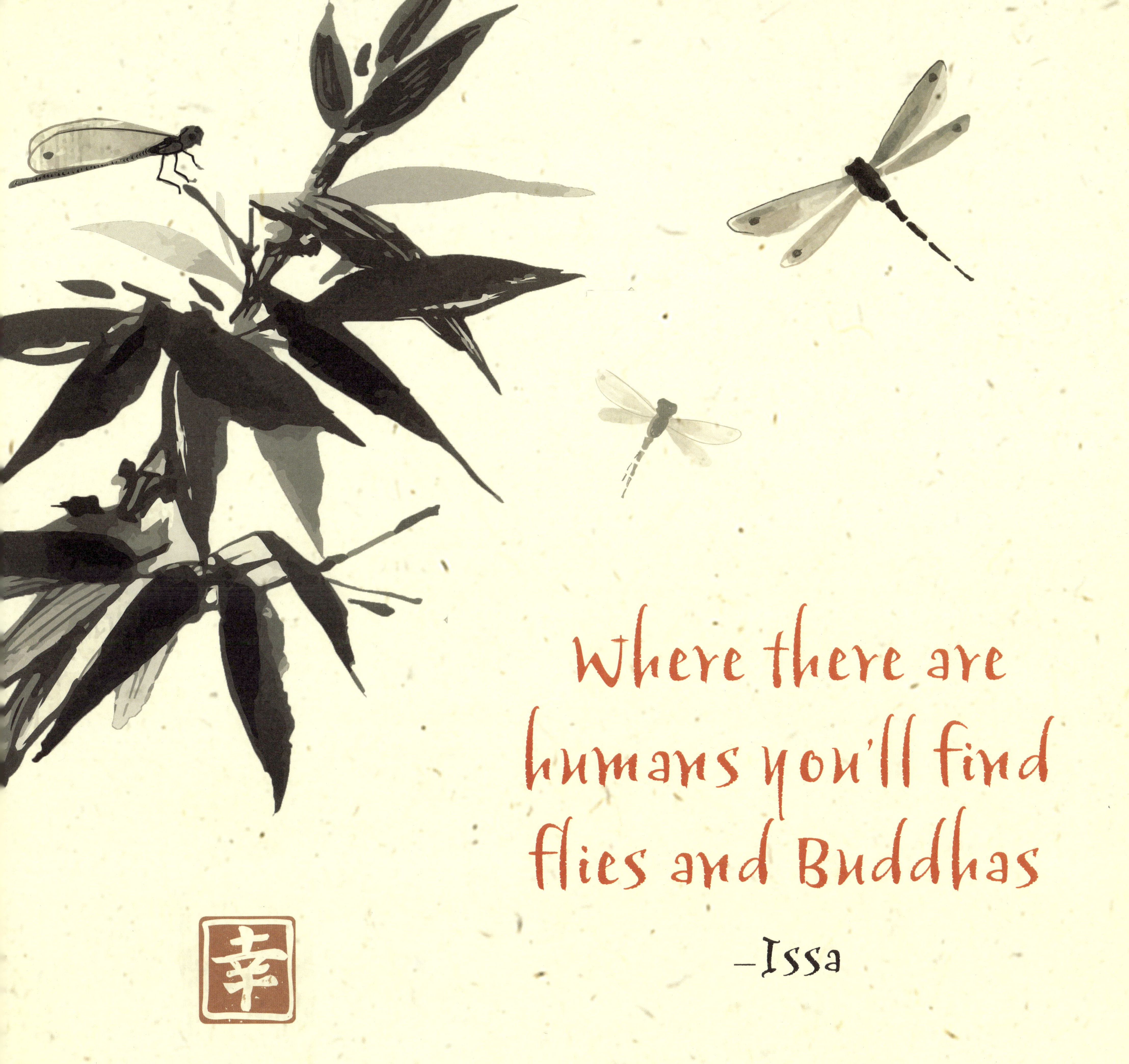

Where there are
humans you'll find
flies and Buddhas

—Issa

Do not follow
in the footsteps
of the wise.
Seek what they
sought.

—Basho

August

2019

Sunday	Monday	Tuesday	Wednesday	Thursday	Friday	Saturday
JULY 2019 S M T W TH F S 1 2 3 4 5 6 7 8 9 10 11 12 13 14 15 16 17 18 19 20 21 22 23 24 25 26 27 28 29 30 31	SEPTEMBER 2019 S M T W TH F S 1 2 3 4 5 6 7 8 9 10 11 12 13 14 15 16 17 18 19 20 21 22 23 24 25 26 27 28 29 30			1	2	3
4	5 Civic Holiday (Canada) Summer Bank Holiday (Scotland)	6	7	8	9	10
11 Eid al-Adha begins at sundown	12	13	14	15	16	17
18	19	20	21	22	23	24
25	26 Summer Bank Holiday (Eng., Wales, N. Ire.)	27	28	29	30	31 Islamic New Year begins at sundown

When hungry, eat your rice.
When tired, close your eyes.
Fools may laugh at me but wise
men will know what I mean.

—Lin-chi

September 2019

Sunday	Monday	Tuesday	Wednesday	Thursday	Friday	Saturday
1	2 Labor Day	3	4	5	6	7
8 Grandparents Day	9	10	11	12	13	14
15	16	17	18	19	20	21 International Day of Peace
22	23 Queen's Birthday (WA Australia)	24	25	26	27	28
29 Rosh Hashanah begins at sundown	30					

AUGUST 2019

S	M	T	W	Th	F	S
				1	2	3
4	5	6	7	8	9	10
11	12	13	14	15	16	17
18	19	20	21	22	23	24
25	26	27	28	29	30	31

OCTOBER 2019

S	M	T	W	Th	F	S
		1	2	3	4	5
6	7	8	9	10	11	12
13	14	15	16	17	18	19
20	21	22	23	24	25	26
27	28	29	30	31		

October 2019

Sunday	Monday	Tuesday	Wednesday	Thursday	Friday	Saturday
		1	2	3	4	5
6	7 Labour Day (ACT, NSW & SA Australia) Queen's Birthday (QLD Australia)	8 Yom Kippur begins at sundown	9	10	11	12 Traditional Columbus Day
13	14 Columbus Day Observed Thanksgiving (Canada)	15	16	17	18	19
20	21	22	23	24	25	26
27	28 Labour Day (New Zealand)	29	30	31 Halloween		

SEPTEMBER 2019

S	M	T	W	Th	F	S
1	2	3	4	5	6	7
8	9	10	11	12	13	14
15	16	17	18	19	20	21
22	23	24	25	26	27	28
29	30					

NOVEMBER 2019

S	M	T	W	Th	F	S
					1	2
3	4	5	6	7	8	9
10	11	12	13	14	15	16
17	18	19	20	21	22	23
24	25	26	27	28	29	30

Walk as if you are kissing the earth with your feet. —Thich Nhat Hanh

November 2019

Sunday	Monday	Tuesday	Wednesday	Thursday	Friday	Saturday
OCTOBER 2019 (see below)	DECEMBER 2019 (see below)				1	2
3 U.S. Daylight Saving Time ends at 2:00 a.m.	4	5 Election Day	6	7	8	9 Mawlid an-Nabi begins at sundown
10	11 Veterans Day Remembrance Day (Canada)	12	13	14	15	16
17	18	19	20	21	22	23
24	25	26	27	28 Thanksgiving	29	30

OCTOBER 2019

S	M	T	W	Th	F	S
		1	2	3	4	5
6	7	8	9	10	11	12
13	14	15	16	17	18	19
20	21	22	23	24	25	26
27	28	29	30	31		

DECEMBER 2019

S	M	T	W	Th	F	S
1	2	3	4	5	6	7
8	9	10	11	12	13	14
15	16	17	18	19	20	21
22	23	24	25	26	27	28
29	30	31				

In this very breath that we take now lies the secret that all great teachers try to tell us.

—Peter Matthiessen

Zen in its essence
is the art of seeing
into the nature of
one's being, and it
points the way
from bondage
to freedom.
–D.T. Suzuki

December 2019

Sunday	Monday	Tuesday	Wednesday	Thursday	Friday	Saturday
1	2	3	4	5	6	7
8	9	10	11	12	13	14
15	16	17	18	19	20	21
22 Hanukkah begins at sundown	23	24	25 Christmas	26 Kwanzaa Boxing Day	27	28
29	30	31				

NOVEMBER 2019

S	M	T	W	Th	F	S
					1	2
3	4	5	6	7	8	9
10	11	12	13	14	15	16
17	18	19	20	21	22	23
24	25	26	27	28	29	30

JANUARY 2020

S	M	T	W	Th	F	S
			1	2	3	4
5	6	7	8	9	10	11
12	13	14	15	16	17	18
19	20	21	22	23	24	25
26	27	28	29	30	31	

“Do not follow in the footsteps of the wise. Seek what they sought.” —Basho

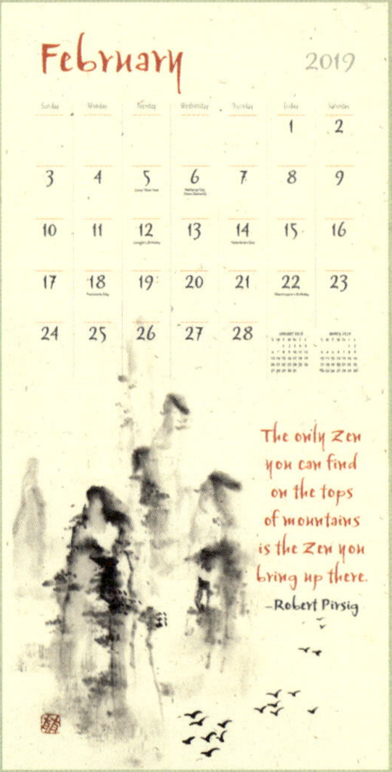

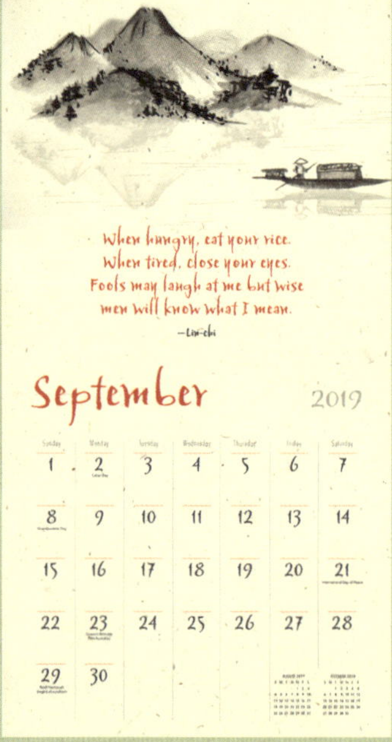

December 2019

Celebrate the visual harmony of Zen. Printed on uncoated stock that recalls calligraphic scrolls, radiant nature photographs are paired with ink drawings—of marshes and birds; dragonflies and mountains—and with words of clarity, insight, and, of course, paradox from Zen sages: *“The meaning of life is to see.”* —Huineng.

$14.99 US / $19.99 CAN. / $25.00 AUS.
Printed in South Korea

Workman Publishing Co., Inc.
225 Varick Street
New York, NY 10014
pageaday.com

workman